A Rose A Day

A Book Of Sacred Rose Prayers

by
Christine Henderson Ph.D

www.roseseichim.com

Disclaimer

This book on personal growth is designed to exercise the mind and free the imagination. The contents are meant to provide a series of options for the reader to self-assess possible ways of enhancing their current life-style.

The contents are not intended as a substitute for the advice of a trained health professional. Please consult your health professional first before applying any of the book's suggestions.

Photos by Lynette Hill

This book is available at Amazon.com & www.roseseichim.com

Dedication

To my dear friend Heather

Who is a guiding light to so many people.

Thank you for reminding me of the power of prayer!

Other Books By Dr Cris Henderson

A Work of Faith
"The History of The Glennie School, Toowoomba"

Cancer Help - written with Angela Raymond
(Simon & Schuster, 1990)

Seichim: the Magic of Seichim Energy Training **

Reiki Inside Out **

Rose Alchemy **

Mini Meditations **

** available for download from www.roseseichim.com

Table of Contents

Foreword

I have always loved roses and when my son William passed over at the age of three some amazing things began to happen with roses.

William had a small amount of money in his bank account so I decided to buy a rose to plant in his memory. I was drawn to a rose called Paradise which I bought. It is a beautiful rose two tone mauve and delicately fragranced. Over the years this rose would flower on special days, his anniversary, his birth, Mothers' Day, my birthday. On his 12th birthday there were 12 roses. The rose had to be replaced and the next one flowered again on special days. I have moved now and recently I happened to be at our local hardware and saw some roses. I thought the only one I need is Paradise, so my hand went straight to a rose, and there it was, the only one they had - so I have planted it in the garden.

My son's girlfriend Amanda passed over about 8 years ago; there was a Paradise rose out for her funeral which I put with her. Amanda's family found a rose called Amanda which was shipped from Western Australia to the east coast. It was quite a rare rose so I took loving care of it nurturing this rose. It began flowering in October 2006. The rose is a bright yellow and as it opens the colour changes to shades of yellow then to an apricot colour. On William's birthday 23rd November 2006, he would have been 20 years old; it was also just one week before the first anniversary of Amanda's passing. As I looked at one of the buds I noticed the shape of two of the centre petals. They were shaped in two perfect hearts!!!! How amazing, it seemed to be a message to me that two precious loved ones were sending me their love via a rose!!! The rose flowered for a few more years after that but never again were there two heart shaped petals.

All during my life I have been presented with roses at different times and many amazing things have happened. They are a gift full of love, perfect in every way.

This beautiful book of rose prayers has been written with love by my dear friend Cris. As you read it may the prayers bring you blessings of love and peace within your essential self.

May you share the wisdom with your loved ones.

Lynette Hill

Acknowledgements

Sincere thanks to all who have helped with the creation, inspiration and publication of this book. The rose sisters live all over the world and continually inspire me to write about the nature and role of the sacred rose.

Thank you to Linda, a true rose sister, who read the manuscript and gave such valuable feedback. Thank you to those who inspired the original poems, most particularly to Beryl, my Rose Mother. Particular thanks to my friends Susan, Leslina, Firesun, Wiz, Ricki, Monic, Monica, Ann and Altea for always being willing to discuss the content of the book. Thank you to Miriam for understanding the inspiration of the rose. Thank you to Hendo, my dear husband, for helping me to keep on writing. Thank you to Dee for reminding me of the true value of my work. Thank you to Trevor for book design and publication. Thank you to Cho for your special contribution and belief in the sacred rose. The beautiful roses that illustrate this book were photographed by my friend Lynette Hill.

For the presence of all of you in my life I am truly grateful.

Cris Henderson
www.roseseichim.com

Introduction

The roses laughed with joy
As they shared their petals with the world
They danced and sang
Their fragrance was released
And all who watched
In that precise moment
Were healed!

Cris Henderson

At the time that the idea of this book came to me I was looking for a prayer book that I could use to help a friend who was experiencing difficulties in his life. None that I found appealed so it was that I decided to write my own prayers in order to make a direct contribution to his well-being. The prayers that I wrote for him helped to change outcomes. Consequently I decided to write more prayers to help other people and subsequently to create a book which would make the prayers more widely available.

There are different ways to use this book. Use one poem a day as a statement of intention or in prayerful form and work your way through the whole book; open the book at random and see which prayer calls to you; or simply ask each day for what you require and see what miracles and magic the rose prayers can facilitate in your life. Later you may decide to repeat the poems in whatever order seems right for you. Perhaps dedicating the month to increasing the levels of peace and harmony in your life will help amplify the rose energy. The dedication can be to anything you wish, whatever is relevant in your life at the time.

The rose angels and archangels are ever ready to help us. They are only waiting to receive a clear request. Once the rose angelic beings receive a lucid appeal it enables them to take action to help us! So think of this special 33 days as your own private time, a period you deserve to have away from the stresses and strains of everyday living.

The rose prayers assist in the development of personal creativity, thereby stimulating individuality and innovation.[1] Utilising them brings out a sense of inner trust which helps the participant to bypass the rational mind and to journey to the central core of being. The sacred poems provide a platform for improving health, happiness and general well being. Recording your experiences in a special diary is just one way to chart the changes. Another way is to develop a book of drawings, or cut-outs, which link to the prayers. After a time the brain begins to accept what it sees as reality and gradually the changes begin to manifest.

If it is not possible for you to remember the words of the poems in a general sense when you close your eyes, then make your own recording and listen to the cadence of the words. Or simply read the sequence three times, then close your eyes and

---

[1] For further information please see Creative Journeys Chapter 8 of 'Dreamgates' by Robert Moss. He studies the conditions for creative flow and what he calls 'creative incubation.' (p.142 New York, Three Rivers Press, 1998 0 609 80216 X. As he explains 'high' creativity is almost always associated with 'high gifts of visualization and receptiveness to visual images.' Ibid. p. 143.

let the poem take you to somewhere that is absolutely your own sacred space.

If you believe in the power of the rose prayers they will certainly make a positive difference in your life. Everyone who feels so inclined can choose to experience the beauty of life, the comfort of roses and the energy of expansiveness.
And most of all – enjoy the journey!

What is the Rose Energy?

The sacred rose energy is a gentle yet powerful symbolic energy based on the energy of the rose, its scent, its form and its nature. The rose is a living entity in its own right. It represents peace, generosity of spirit and gratitude in all their myriad forms. The rose makes a perfect best friend. Its energy is closely linked with the divine feminine and the magnificence of the rose energy often comes into one's life when least expected – especially at a time when help may be needed.

There is a special body of ancient esoteric wisdom which secures and protects the energy of the rose. To understand its mystery is to comprehend the quintessence of the universe. When I began to learn about the rose energy I dreamt about roses and their associated meanings. I learnt to meditate and then began to share my sacred journeying with others. My pilgrimage continues.

The creation and handing on of prayers and poetry was once a celebrated affair, highly valued in so-called primitive societies. Today that sacredness is being revived. Those who have an interest in legends participate in the creation of new forms of expression simply by adding their interest and involvement to the mix. Each shared prayer or poem becomes a declaration of intention, an affirmation or a creative visualization, which, as it is subject to endless repetition, may initiate greater participation in our energetic world.

The unconscious mind is uncharted territory; its existence is understood but most of the time we only know a mere fraction of what goes on there. What we do know is that the greatest journey one can ever take is the journey to the very centre of one's being. The real journey that we are all required to take is this journey of integration, self-realisation and fulfilment - the journey inwards, the journey to the centre of the soul. Should you take the time to complete this series of rose prayers you may find that a number of subtle, sometimes barely perceptive shifts have occurred in your consciousness and that you have travelled a long way on your journey through the world of imagination and freedom. Working in this way brings out a sense of inner trust and wonder bypassing the rational mind and helping to journey to the absolute central core of one's essential self. This is the home of the rose.

What is Sacred Rose Prayer?

Sacred prayer can be described as an intimate expression of personal religion. In its revived form its purpose remains the same - to link individuals using it to a special ray of energy allied with an intensity of feeling so that they remember their true origins and reclaim their sacred power.   When this conjunction takes place the energy often changes for the better, particularly if you decide to use the poems as declarations to reclaim all aspects of who you really are in your totally unlimited form.

This is the purpose behind the creation of the rose poems.

Sacred rose poetry is active affirmation
and each person will react to it differently.

And so, the following sacred poetry is presented to you.

Thank you for giving me the opportunity to write for you.

The Entry Point to the Sacred Rose

Remember when you connect with the rose energy you are only limited by the extent of your imagination.

Become a small version of yourself and walk into the rose, right into its heart – I am with you and so are the rose angels and archangels. Enter into the heart of the rose with us. Use the rose to absorb all your negative emotions, all your feelings and emotions, all your limiting points of view, all those elements that you wish to transform and even some you seem unwilling to let go. Ask for the intervention of the sacred rose into your life on a daily basis.

All of a sudden as we stand in the middle of the rose it begins to spin. The rose turns around more and more quickly and becomes like a kaleidoscope. The colours change. You perceive that the rose is all colours – you are as one with the magnificent possibilities that represent these colours. It is an amazing feeling to tap into the sense of excitement that this spinning sensation brings. It becomes so fast that it is like the energy of a whirling dervish. Round and around it goes, faster and faster, spinning and cleansing, clearing and changing. There are three of us in the centre of the rose. Your special rose angel stands with you as your guide and supporter and so do I. The rose angel seems so pleased to see you here. As the spinning intensifies some petals fall away taking any of your rigid points of view with them. You may want to take this opportunity to have a quiet conversation with her as the spinning rose world slows and the vibrations settle. You can ask all your questions at this point.

Finally the experience comes to an end and it is time for you to return to your home base. You may wish to rest for a time and to remember all that you have seen on your special rose journey.

The sacred rose can be re-activated whenever you require access to its essence. Each time it reappears in front of you it will be in its full form, the petals gleaming and waiting to receive your discards! Repeat this process as many times as you wish in order to transform all unwanted energy – and to ensure that it leaves you permanently. There is an unlimited supply of rose energy and so each time the sacred rose is used it returns gleaming and shining and inviting you to release more. It is, after all, a living symbol. It is alive. It has its own consciousness. You have been given the special entry way to enable full communion with the sacred rose.

When you feel complete and when you have released all that is necessary and then relaxed for a time - please tell your rose angel and she will come into your presence once more. When the rose angel appears she is  *holding another pure rose as a special gift for you – she places the* rose directly into your heart – into the Garden of the Heart and here this divine rose will flourish – it will spread the rose energy through your veins and transfer it into your blood. It will open your heart to experience a new paradigm in which imagination and creativity are welcomed and honoured. Never underestimate the power of the sacred rose.

Heart of Roses

In my dreams roses surround me in an aura of calm.
I send them to you with my love.
I take you to the Dream Field where roses abound.
Let us travel there now in our essence
and view the roses.
They are everywhere in every colour, wonderful
beautiful living entities these roses.
The roses in the Dream Field
will nurture and love and support you.
Take them into your body mind and spirit,
indeed into your soul,
Honour yourself
and the divine energy of the rose.
You awake to the dawn of a new day
filled with new energy and divine possibility.
And so do I!

The Daily Pattern of the Rose

On my return route to Sirius now, planet of my birthing, I ignite my luminous body from the acceptance of my divinity. From within the vastness of my inner Sun, I birth potential worlds. I release myself from my own stronghold. I give myself permission to stop hiding. As I lower all barriers my cells vibrate with rising intuition. I yearn for more.

My personal Tree of Life glistens with anticipation, love and unadulterated power. Its roses blossom into rainbows and reach out into the sky. Within the foundation of my human form I awaken my star essence, touching gently all worlds and all beings. Feathers caress my inner and outer being. My inner Sun blazes with unconditional love. I feel the radiance of my embodied Moon. I taste its brilliance. I send a feather to reawaken you.

I call the Rose Archangels to me. The time is now.

Part One

Part One of the Rose Prayers opens the door to the Rose Energy. It brings with it a taste of the sacred rose and how knowledge of its vibration can alter daily situations for the better and engender vibrant well-being with the greatest of ease. Many of the poems in this section were inspired as I worked with my husband as he recovered from a debilitating stroke. I observed the courage which he instinctively used to transform his situation. I remain inspired by his intention to proceed to full health.

Day 1: The Rose Angel

My hands fold in front of me
As I assume the attitude of prayer
I link now with you
You who are in my thoughts right now
As you wonder what to do
And how you can rise from this situation
The one in which you find yourself
I watch from afar
And send you my love
At first this is all I think I can do
Yet suddenly my intention magnifies
It takes form so quickly I am amazed
I feel the warmth of a presence
Right next to me
I look up into the eyes
Of an enormous rose angel
Her head is covered in a halo
Of scented roses
Her perfume wafts towards my upturned face
I inhale it and relax
My prayers are handed over
To the beauty of you, Rose Angel
You will visit my friend today
And reassure him
That you will be with him
Now and always!
I stand aside now
And know that it is done.

Day 2: The Rose Fairies

Tonight you hesitate to go to sleep
You are perturbed and wondering
If restfulness will come
Or will the dreams of the past
Chase you down the time line
Pursuing you until you cry out
Stop and leave me be you shout!
You are adrift
In the memories of sadness
And you feel so alone
Just call out now and ask
And fairy friends will come in the night
To love and support you
They come in droves once invited
Your room filled with their wonder and delight
As they regard you
You who really understands them
And know just who they are
One of the few of those
Who remember them from past days
When you all played together
In your childhood
When no-one told you that fairies did not exist
When you were free to believe
Your own special truth
When you knew the Fairy Kingdom
Thrived
And that rose fairies were available
To help you
To walk between the worlds!

Walk this way again
And bring their essence together with yours
And at last be healed!

Day 3: Gentling

Restricted no more
You awake to the bright fuzz
Of a new day
Filled with golden opportunities

Your day dawns calmly
You feel contented
As you watch the skies
For portents
All that comes is
A sense of deep abiding calm
A rose glow surrounds you
As you gently receive
This brand new day
Gentling your energy
Expanding your vibration
Never minimizing it
Stepping out joyfully
Into the rose light!

Day 4: Regeneration

The day eddies around a new you
With a smile upon your lips
You lie enchanted
Resting in your bed
With memories of recent hours
Filled with unexpected laughter
And a sense of joyous expectation
Bubbling up inside you
You realise that in such a short time
You have travelled from the deepest sense of gloom
To something spectacular
A release of sorts
This sparkling life that is opening before you
Shows infinite possibilities
You are no longer dismayed
You feel the essence of the rose
Blossoming inside your body
And you know
You are transformed!

Day 5: A Room Full Of Roses

Wherever you may be today
And whatever you are doing
Imagine my friend
Your room is full of roses
Perhaps your car, your bus, your train,
Perhaps your street, your office, your home
Yet certainly your room

The roses sit one on top of the other
Clustering closely
They send scents so pure
Your atmosphere is cleansed and purified
You open your nostrils
And inhale the sensation
of pure pink, rampant red and yearning yellow
The scents assail you
They open you to perfect balance
And to perfect health and well-being

You gentle yourself into pleasantness,
no pain and perfect purification
You feel hopelessly happy
You do not know why
No alien scents for you
No impurities in the atmosphere
Only roses raining their gentle essence on you
As they cling to your personal being
Sacrificing nothing
Enhancing everything

And so today -
And every day
I wish you well
And a room full of roses!

Day 6: Dainty Feet

Your dainty feet
Have trodden many miles
Walked many journeys
Over and over
Your dainty feet
Are subsumed with signs of activity
And we are mindful
Of the miles they have covered
Call to your dainty feet now
Toes of Destiny
Transform
Toes of Destiny
Transform
Be upstanding in your rose healing
Flatten and sense the nuances
Of Mother Earth
Absorb her energies
See the toes open now
Without anxiety
In other lives they may have been
Burnt or mistreated
Tortured even
No more pain now
In this life they can be free
And plant themselves firmly
On the ground
Stretch them out now
Open them to Mother Earth
And know that your vibration
Rises above mortal ills

And aches and pains
And that you are infinite,
Your new feet are part of all that is.
Look at them now
Direct a stream of pure love through them
Into the greatness of Mother Earth
Know that they will carry you many more miles
And that they are your friends forever.
Climb onto your feet now and try them out.
Test them on the ground
See how supportive and loving they are.
They will walk you into the new rose paradigm
As your true self, a rose goddess
And if perchance you observe that they are tired
Call the rose angels to you
And ask them to take you
Wherever you need to be
And they will.

Day 7: Divine Rose Energy

Our day flows in harmony
With heavenly rhythm
The rhythm is like
Gentle waves
Lapping on the sand
In time with the heartbeat
Of Mother Earth
All will be moved
Into the flow of Divine Rose Order
That you choose to create
I ask for you to be connected
To the rhythm of the sacred rose
And once more with feeling
Divine Order
Enters the River of Life
And flows creatively
From the Circle of Light
To us individually
And then into the blood stream
Of the Earth Mother herself
To effect healing
To you, to me
And to all the world
And so it is.

Day 8: Fairy Breath

The breath of generations of fairy beings
Combines to bless you
Sons and Daughters of the fairies
You are filled with their talents
You dance and sing
You make music and you chant for them
They work with you endlessly
Blessing all your endeavors
They play with you
At night time in your dreams
And you cavort amongst the stars
With your fairy sisters and brothers
And come back here each morning
With their music ringing in your ears
The scent of roses
Is in your nostrils when you wake
You look beyond the clouds
You see things that others cannot
You are part gypsy too
Fey and almost wild
Walking between two worlds
And beyond them
You take the essence of your template
You weave from your magical eyes
And plant the results here on earth
For all of us
And we love you!

Day 9: Your Sacred Spine

Your spine tingles and vibrates in anticipation
As you stretch it, moving gently
A door opens within it
A door to your imagination
You find yourself journeying
Inside your spine
You feel your spinal fluid
It flows like a river
In one instant you decide
And you jump in
You canoe along your spine
Up and down you move
Looking into the crevices
and commandeering its tidal flow
You access power sources
Previously closed to you
You journey relentlessly
Up and down, to and fro
On your Rose River of Life
You see the form and structure
Of your spine begin to change
All damage is gradually reversed
As you have chosen wholeness
You actualize your vital force
From your gentle spirit
And it emerges into your Rose River of Life
Your body releases its pain
And you bring the energy
Of infinite possibility
Into your life!

Day 10: The Blue Light

The blue light has come at last
And the first phase is done
The blue light has come at last
So now we can be one!
Leave it all behind you
The pressure and the pain
Leave it all behind you
And heal your lovely frame!
Give thanks for your helpers
The Goddess of the Rose
Say thank you to Mother Earth
As you begin your earthly role
Living as you were meant to do
Has helped to heal her soul
As you clear the way
The children of the light
Travel in from Heaven
To overcome the night
Say thank you to your shamans
They are visible at last
They transform your work to starlight
They never were typecast
Use your new rose energy
To help you on your way
You have work to do tomorrow
And you have so much to say
In transforming your grieving
At last you beat the pain
You bring light to everyone
So no one is the same

And as you clean the portals
This is what you are here to do
You bring to earth the rose form
A form you always knew.
The blue light has come at last
And the first phase is done
The blue light has come at last
So now we can be one!

Day 11: Choice

Energetic promises emerge
As your sacred rose unfolds inside your heart
Now that we are no longer separate
Wounded healers no more
A gift to ourselves and to the world
We never knew about
What can we achieve together?
A universal family working harmoniously
We are all gifts
To the consciousness of this place,
This planet
Know your greatness now
All the energy you have tried
To eliminate from your world, to decimate
All the small safeness you have sought to hide securely
Becomes available as the essence of pure possibility
You are a drawing as yet undrawn
One brought to life
As you choose
In whatever form you say
You are invited to take your place
In this creation
As a Master of Energy
Will you take up
This magnificent suggestion?
Will you rise to this occasion?
Will you choose differently?
Will you enter through the gleaming gates
Of your Rose Kingdom now?
Will you be healed?

Day 12: The Key To The Kingdom

Take down your mask
Lower your barriers slowly and gently
Into the warmth of the Earth Mother
Open your eyes, your face, yes even your mouth
Look around you at the new day
Be receptive, grateful
Receive everything
Judge nothing
Reignite your generosity of spirit
And welcome roses into your life
I am you, you are me
The barriers are down
I am the key
The key handed to you now
I am large, bold, brassy, bossy
Your key
Your key to the kingdom of you
You receive me
You look at me
You contact me moving all over
To see what such a key feels like
You generate waves in the air
As you signal me
I change
One moment I am
Large, old, ancient, antique almost
Yet another
I am generous in all my proportions
Bright, shiny, pretty, preposterous
You look and look at me

Taking your time
Making me wait
Oh come on now, I cry
You have had time
You have had space
You have had everything you need
Get on now - do it I say - be it- speak it
Get on
And suddenly as if you hear me
You open your hassled heart
You touch it with the key
You turn, you open the door
You walk in
And nothing is ever the same again.

Day 13: The Golden Ladder Of Light

The sensuous strength
Of Mother Earth
Pushes up at you
To where you sit
In a sacred spot
Once beloved
By the Rainbow Serpent
Oh Sister and Brother mine
Drawn here
Through many trials and tribulations
Until you are finally
In a place where you are meant to be
Nestling into the red and golden earth
Centering yourself as you find the core
Of your special destiny, your sacred rose.
Long have we spoken of where and why
And now at least we know.
Go bring in the ladder
The Golden Ladder of Light
Hold on tightly now
As the rose angels
Climb down the ladder to where you stand
Look up in rapt awe
At the sight
The pathway you have created
Between Heaven and Earth
Is simply glorious
Oh Sister and Brother mine
You have opened a sacred line
With your heart felt healing

The pain, the sorrow and the core of you
You have cracked a cloud!
Opening it to the divine
Within you
Oh Sister and Brother mine
You have done it
And down the ladder they come
The most glorious array
Of dazzling beings ever seen
Oh Sister and Brother mine
Greet the rosy ones
Make them welcome and open your heart
You are in the company
Of like minded beings
You are safe and secure
You have created Sacred Space, a pathway
Between Heaven and Earth.
Specially chosen for this task
And now truly able
To glory in it
You have surrendered and succeeded
And now is the time
For joyous thoughts
And as the rosy ones flow down the ladder
You remember your true home
And you know who you really are
You remember that the stars are you
And you are at once one with them
And the essence of glorious possibility
Is this day released through our reunion
Onto Mother Earth!

Day 14: Cellular Memories

Our covenant is ready for clearing
The key has been handed down
The choice made
For us to open if we will
The door to a perfect future
Why are we waiting?
What is it that holds us here
Fixed in an imperfect reality
Stretching and straining our bodies
Into impossible commitments
Tiring ourselves as we search for a solution
To our daily round of seeming tests
Suddenly the sound of a crash lands
Behind us
We turn suddenly terrified and look
We see all of our past destroyed
Wiped out in this single moment
Our terror at making the same mistakes again
Can no longer hold up
There is no past only the present
Only this interval
In which we are impregnated
With the sense of possibility and passion
Twin flames of our new existence
Energies of rose consciousness
Striking us now
And bringing us into total awareness
In this one pure moment of time.

Day 15: Generosity

Generous you
You have given your rose essence
To those in need
For centuries
As we have played hide and seek
With our intrinsic selves
You have harboured us
As we ran from the peril in our lives
Into the haven of your presence
We have seen new possibilities
You have kicked and cajoled us
Into being infinite
And most of all
You have held the space
For us to change
Generous you!

Day 16:   Falling Roses

Roses fall from the sky
As I look through my window
And I think I am dreaming
They cover a small patch
Of Mother Earth outside
I hear myself
Draw in my breath
A sharp intake
As the downfall continues
The magic intensifies
As the rose petals
Dance on the ground
Outside my house
Interfacing with the Earth Mother
They form generous shapes
And symbols
And I am amazed
My heart opens at this sight
And the rose energy
Ignites my sacred space
I am alone no more
Bereft no more
I am now conscious
Of all that I can be
And I choose that
My choice
Made here and now
As the rose petals
Continue their Dance of Love
On one spot

On Mother Earth
And bring with them
Their illumination
Their sacredness
Their joy!

Day 17: Weeping

I weep with you
As the day begins
And the pain returns
Pushing you to the edge
Of your endurance
You open your eyes
Your anger immense
It boils out of your body
I watch it leave you
The red pall swarming above you
I know that something
Must be done to help now
I call the Rose Archangels
They respond immediately
Blowing into your room
Gorgeous roses flow
From their wings as they enter
They smile lovingly at you
And you see them and respond
And the pain leaves your body
Never to return!

Day 18: Star Mountain Sage

You are weaving new emblems now
Star Mountain Sage
Your emblems wander
Easily and gently
Through to the heavens
Where they lodge harmoniously
As pure rose energy
Delectable and delightful
Where the promises they make
Enhance our futures
Giving us harmony in the heavens
You are the dream weaver elect
The keeper of that dream
And the Star Mountain Sage herself
From your eerie
You select the right dreams
For the right person
You connect with their Tree of Life
And spin rainbow rose colours right at it
Until the connection is made
As you do you feel the strength
Of your commitment
And all your days
Are happy
Your new freedom
Transports you to your optimism and power
Your pulse the dream
Until it clambers down the Tree
Mother Wind energises
The dream enters the earthly realm

And reaches its intended
You are blessed by all those
With whom you work
Our Star Mountain Sage
Lives are illuminated by your dream
Now revere your inheritance
And move forward in one swelling flowing movement
So that all will be well on Mother Earth!

Day 19: A Special Thought For Today

I saw you walk away
You left your sweet smile
It stayed with me
For such a long while
I turned for home
Thinking all the while
That you were alone
Perhaps it would be
A miracle it is true
If you could somehow meet
A Rose Angel or even two
I asked for the Rose Angels to come in to play
To be with you daily
And to help you make your way
I know they are helping you
And with you they will stay
They will be there for you
Through thick and through thin
Do not ever give up
And do not ever give in
Simply call out and say
'I know you are there
If you can hear me at all
Just please touch my hair.'
An answer will come
And this I will share
It will help you so much
It will make you aware
Of the power of you
Of your divinity and flair

Of your infinite self
And the way that you care!

Day 20: Moving On The Web Of Life

Your Web of Life
Floats now
Freefalling through the light
Mystified you watch
As it sits quietly without movement
Its shape discernible
You know now
That it is time
For movement in your life
Choices delight you
Your language becomes poetic
As you watch and listen
For new signs
You observe intently
You have an ancient urge
To poke at your web
To make it move
To have something happen
To be interactive
Once more in control
And you realise that is not the way
Wishing now
To move and change and grow
Loving your body intensely
You sit quietly and reminisce
Looking back down your timeline
To all those lives
Now left behind
When you disregarded your body
Almost regretting it

When your rose spirit life
Was totally separate
From your earthly form
When all you wanted
Was to follow your rose spirit
And leave this earth
Let us review
This pattern
And see if you are
Doing it all again
Only you can decide
Make a choice
And whatever it is
Be generative, joyful,
Creative and expansive
Feel the energy flow
And now if you have changed
Your point of view
Feel free to blow on your web
With warm breath
Until it begins to move
At long last
She is alive again
Your Rose Web
Moving and gyrating
Gently opalescent
Bringing change and expansion
Opening to the new

Day 21: Silent Witness

I am awake now
Watching for rose angels
On this auspicious day
The sun is bright and glittering
Like a jewel in the heavens
And then I hear it
I hear the fluttering of the heavenly host
A subtle definitive sound
On the airways
As their wings move collectively
In absolute co-ordination
Sending a breeze through me
Into my essence
And coursing through my veins and arteries
Calming my restlessness

As they pass
They bend to kiss my bowed head
Their sweetness permeates the air
And then they are gone
They are simply the precursors
Introducing Lord Michael
Who beams in now
Imperious yet loving
Demanding yet gentle
Huge, violet and golden, shining
Bringing a mighty presence
Into my space
Flapping enormous wings
And making the furniture shake in his presence

A Book Of Rose Prayers

I begin to cry yet again
It is too hard, too much
I begin to protest
As his burning eyes bore through my reservations
His lightning flash is so golden
My eyes stream with more tears
He is waiting for my answer
He is allowing me to come to my senses
And to acknowledge him
His imperious brow is raised
It is his eyes that melt my resolve
They are almond and amber both
Curious and gorgeous in their intensity
Suddenly I have no choice
I cannot fight any more
I cannot seek to walk away from this wonder
I have to walk on in the light
I surrender
I surrender totally and absolutely
For all time
And for all of us down through the ages
This then is the day of the integration
The day of the new and old
And now it comes again
Flowing on the wind
The melody so sweet and mournful
That the rose angels ceased
The beating of their wings
And quieted in ecstasy

The scent of roses
Gently wafts through my home

Smiles like sunlight rays
Bloom upon my cheeks
I wait here expectantly
And my day is glorious!

Day 22: Fairy Feet

My toes tingle
My feet curve and stretch
They ascertain my future
Almost before I do
They point me in a new direction
They look up at me and laugh
They touch the earth
In special places
Leaving the essence of my imprint
They tease me often
I give them special names
As I do now for different parts
Of my body

I've done this before of course
In other lives at other times
I have used you to run and jump
To leap over walls
To run towards a lover
To leave situations of pain
And discomfort
To tremble at my despair
And to twinkle in hopefulness
To wander in the petals of roses
Fairy feet I christen you now
These special names
And as I do
You draw yourselves
Into a bundle then relax
Pronounce yourself ready

And walk to the Rose Gate
Of new freedom
And take me through
Living luxuriously
Leaving the old behind
And renewed and robust
I take in this different place
And begin my new life
With joyful expansive expectation!

Day 23: Geraldines

Geraldines emerge as a group from the ocean
Glowing, green luminous iridescent
Their beauty is sensational
Long hair gleaming eyes
Rose angels advancing in unison
Large wings that can be extended
Or withdrawn in an instant
The touch of their tips provides instant healing
Chameleon like
They gather on the shore
Whilst we of the ancient lineage
Observe our new compatriots
With great interest and joy
They have come from
The crack between the worlds
Our physical world
And our major parallel universe
Sashaying in
The heavens blaze with fire
At this momentous event
And our world
Is transformed
By these rose angels
The celestial goddesses of light
In graceful care
Crying blood red roses
As they meet us
Their palace on an island
In the marshy land of Avalon
Was only for the initiates

That life has melted thawed and dissolved
The aerial agents of holy inspiration
Have brought them here
To claim their rightful inheritance
For we are them
And they are us
The ancient and the modern
The old and the new
Conjoined at last
And now may this new Avalon rise
An island of luminosity
Where the goddesses thrive
In a new golden age
And so it is!

Day 24: Touching Wings

I touch your wings
With my wing tips
As we stand in the circle
Of sacred rose fire
I watch you transform
And I am inspired
Your vitality zings
Through the Rose Web of Life
Your creativity blossoms
You inspire others
To go through the hard times
As you have
And emerge victorious!

Day 25: The Lustre Of The Rose

The lustre of the rose
Enters the room
It gravitates towards me
Climbing the walls
And the rose portal opens
In front of me
In the corridor
My eyes widen
The energy drifts towards me
Approaching faster now
Nearer and nearer
Closer and closer
And everything seems right
The lustre of the rose expands
Enveloping us in its pure fragrance
Wonderful roses
You open the energy
Of the night
You generate life
You perpetuate
Liveliness
In bringing back together
All the pieces of me
That have been used
To fracture my consciousness
My energy expands now
My joy intensifies
And I walk forward
Into forever!

Day 26: Solitude

I sheltered you
From the storm
When you were in need
I basked in the sunshine
With roses
That you generated
On my behalf
I shielded you
I protected you
I was your calm
From the storm
You walked into wellness
Into the endless energy
That I created on your behalf
Empty now I release you
To your new life
I wait for someone else to enter
Someone I can shield
From life's storms
Someone who knows
The power of the rose
And yes, they are coming now!
I salute you
I let you go
And watch you walk
Into triumphant success!
Roses surround you
And all is well in your world once more!

Day 27: The Unfurling Of The Rose

The portal is open now
It stands in splendour before us
The energy glows, it flows
Through and beyond
Taking us to our Web of Life
Where we cavort and sing and celebrate
The changes that have finally come
We have released all of the past
And now we celebrate our freedom
With our rose friends and relatives
Who have been our pathfinders and guides
For generations
In our divine capacity as the Rose emissaries
We call the energy to bring healing
To those who are suffering as the change diversifies
We release past fears and know
That there is divine intervention coming now
And we call for that to happen
In the lives of those whom we love
We declare that intervention
Is made physical now
Within the bodies of our pathfinders
And so it is!

Day 28: A Room In Heaven

Today I came across
A room in heaven
I entered warily
And was won over
This room in heaven opened to places
Where I had never been before
It rained roses on my thoughts
And raised them
To dreams of wonder and delight
It held within it
Art and artifacts, ancient and modern
Filled with epicentres of light
That shone right on me
As I walked around
My eyes sucking greedily
As they opened wider and wider
To receive
Extraordinary signals and colour
Vibrant and striking
In paintings ancient and modern
Collages of cumulus clouds
Winking and smiling at me
As I walked faster and faster
Trying to see it all
On and on I went
At each turn in the corridor
Another surprise!

Abandoning all pretense
I ran then

From gallery to gallery
Turning faster and faster
On kaleidoscopes of light
Egyptian figures claimed me
Mexican artifacts danced for me
French furniture and furnishings
From the eighteenth century no less
Cavorted in front of my eyes
Each one better than the one before
Outside the grace filled trees
Bent and swayed as I ran
Keeping time to my frantic
All-embracing jog
Until I found Her at last
I stopped quietly in my tracks
And eyed Her
The Madonna - a rendition so spectacular
That the artist's gift to the world
Dwarfed the others
At least for me
Her form was visible to all
Her sacredness sure and certain
And her sweetness
At last all mine.

Day 29: Dolphins

A school of dolphins gambols out at sea
Above the holy entry to Atlantis
They spot us as we spot them
Seven break off and head our way
Plunging up and down together
Dancing and riding on the waves
Careering alongside our bobbing boat
Glittering electric blue on top shining
Fading at the sides
through to green grey metal dune-like markings
Until they become pure white
They are streamlined and gleaming
From their elegant beaks to their clean-cut tails
Feeding at the sides of our boat through green
Metal coloured dunes as waves glitter
And their complex markings
Glow as pure white.

Beautiful abstraction of speed energy power and light
They leap out of the water in unison
Plunging spirally then vanishing
Like the swift secret shadows of surfers
Materializing again only to soar
Into the air once more in another great wave heralding immense
change

Creating harmony and beauty and synchronicity
In all our energetic interchanges
You draw the sea into you - as they do
You rise strikingly above the ordinary

You know that you can do it alone
Merging the male and female within you
Until the world vibrates with your harmony
And now you have done it –
complete and final you rest and revise
For now you have shown the way
And you are One.

Day 30: Heart Of Roses

A heart of roses

Leaps from my heart

And into the sea

It twirls and whirls

It opens and shuts

Its form and content

It gradually absorbs

The essence of the sea

And as it does

The roses form and reform

They call out to me

Their shape now flowing

They begin to sing

And I sit on the ship

And watch their dance

The mystic light of a rainbow

Suddenly appears

It engages the heart

And fills it with light

And I send it on to you

This heart of roses

To illuminate your day!

Day 31: The Rose Gate

The Rose Gate is opening now
And it is time to step on through
As I make the forward movement
I see I am standing there with you
You, who are my true friend
Come with me now
Let us take this step together
Whilst the gate is still ajar
And the tears they all flow freely
This is such a momentous move
There is nothing left on this side
Nothing that we must prove
We thank the rose energy
For all it has done for us
We move in new dimensions
We expand our living space
We generate rose love
For all those whom we meet
We can heal the world now
We never accept defeat!

Day 32: My Tree Of Life

My Tree of Life is replanted now
Beneath my sacred site, my home
It revels in the levels of intense energy
That has guarded us here
It transforms any pockets of remaining darkness
Into light and life filled cumulus clouds.
Of sanctity love and good fortune
It reflects outwards and deflects mal intent
It reflects inward and shines on the DNA of the house.
Until it sparkles with its own light
It creates the ambience necessary
For fortune to find me
To be my friend and ally
To release the abundance within
Through its roots I connect with
The sacred rose
New rose energies are forged
The rivers flow
My blood family transforms
New friends emerge
And find me
And I am at peace with my Tree of Life.

Day 33: The Hole Into My Part Of Heaven

I sat on the tips of fairy fingers
And felt the brush of these fairy feathers
On my feet
As I reached up towards heaven
The hole to heaven was enlivened
And we danced with joy
As I had come home at last
Come home to heaven
On a bridge made of fairy fingers
Enlivened with fairy breath
I sat still
For a long moment
And gave thanks.

Part Two
Clearing Past Influences

Sometimes certain situations seem familiar to us as if we are in some sort of pattern that keeps going round and round in a loop and repeating itself. If this happens to you use 'Circus, Circus' first and then some of the other poems in this section. You will find these poems will clear the energetic repetition.

Circus, Circus

It is my time in the circus today
I am the star
The attraction to be shown off
And flaunted
The Ring Master watches progress
He is someone I know
In this existence
And I feel the bile rise
Within me
As he pushes me to perform
But here is someone new
Upon the scene
A woman steps from the shadows
Her face shielded from me
I know her
She is the one
Who is to follow me
Down the centuries
Betraying me
Betraying my friendship, my friends and my trust
I see her later at the camp
Pointing at us
With her whip flicking greedily
Left, right, left, right
Die, Live, Die, Live
Her hated tone damages my ears
I see her at the trials
Giving evidence against us
In every incarnation
She is there

And loathing fills my cells
Who am I my intrinsic self
Calls out into the density
Of mixed emotions
Who am I and what am I doing here?
For this is the time
Of the Fall of Atlantis
A brutal male energy has taken hold
And grabbed at my Goddess essence
And supporting him
The perverted female
Has joined the patriarchy
In an unsuccessful attempt to use me
And to wear me down
Into abject nothingness
Not just myself
But all the Sisters of the Rose
Who carry the energy of the Goddess
And so I play the game
I leap and cavort like an animal
Rolling over and over in the sawdust
And bringing myself to my feet
Without undue effort
Because today is the day
Of our escape
It is all planned
My sisters and I rise up as one
And walk steadily towards them
The Ring Master and his cohort
They back away, frightened now,
Withdrawing, then tripping
He bumps his head

She falls into an unconscious spin
We leave as a group
Walking into the water
The cold dark water
Swimming away
Our energies intact
The secrets of the stars
Embodied in our bodies
The men and their distorted consorts
At last on the run
Understanding their peril
We look back with mercy
In our eyes
And agree that transformation
Can come in this life time
We graciously allow
The Brothers of the Rose
To be reborn
Roses cover the scene
And the time is now.

The Well

The lights of Egypt
Shine remorselessly
From the sun
In the bright blue cloudless sky
They touch parched earth
They dance, they sing
As they call you in
You feel the energy
In your physical body
Wondering where and why
We are at your well
And you – guardian goddess
Are being called home
To work your special magic
Worldwide through the wells
You stretch your wings and sing
While we delight
In the insistent energy
Of this special well
The connection is forged now
And your job newly ordered
Take up your crystal wand
And command your landscape
To open to your power
Send new ley lines out
All over Mother Earth
Open the power centres
And crack the codes
Of the Earth Mother
Retrieve your personal crystal skull

From an alcove in your well
And show your glory
To all the world
AND SO IT IS!

Rainbows

Written especially for Christine McCartney, a true Sister of the Rose, who has now gone 'over the rainbow.'

August 2008

If you are working with anyone who is about to go home, this poem will assist you both.

Rainbows gather between us
They glow generously
Baked in our love
They glitter and gleam
Linking our hearts
Making us smile quietly
You are being tortured now
I worry and wonder what to do
And then I realise
I can cross the space between us
And come to you
Relieving your suffering
As I do
When I reach your side
You are unaware
Of my presence
And then I perceive
A faint stirring
In your energy field
Your eyelids flutter
My quiet words
Of rose healing
Cover you like a blanket
They make your energy body
Reignite once more

As you slip away from me
And return home!

The Healing Fields Of Heaven

The Healing Fields are part of the sacred landscape of heaven. Healing in this sacred place brings many advantages as the past present and future in the Fields are as one. Please take a journey here to change your life forever and to continue to clear old patterns.

Janus smiles and turns gently towards you
You press his face
On many points
To open the rose gate
Over and over
Pressing, trying, generating
Changing at last opening
You look before you
At the sacred landscape
Of glorious Heaven
The Healing Fields beyond you
You stand enthralled
Gazing in rapture
At the sight greeting your eyes
The tents are scattered
Seemingly random
An unknown pattern
Across the verdant green
Of the grass
A gentle breeze reaches you
Your eyes fill with tears
You scan the field
And notice the detail
The tents are shaped

Differently
They seem to move and change
As you watch
Your guides surround you
Senior rose archangels
Generous in their efforts
To heal your pain
You step inside
The sacred space
Walking slowly between the tents
Until you find yours
You know it at once
And you enter without pausing
Your safety house
The tent is purple
And the mauve of its essence
Beams directly into your being
Generating peace and joy
The rose archangels
Enter your tent with you
Your healing space
Is now completely safe and private
Rose symbols pulse and vibrate
As your tent is illuminated
With healing rainbows of light
Generous gifts are given
You are surrounded with love
Time passes
The ground rocks
And your healing sojourn
Brings you profound appreciation
Of the wonders of life

You and your sacred escort
Leave now
And you return at once
To Mother Earth
Charged with joy forever
And so it is!

Part Three

Special Prayers For Mothers

All mothers can be called Rose Mothers – all mothers embody the nurturing that comes from the rose – all mothers generate healing. There is one mother who is special – these poems were originally written for her – my other

mother Beryl – and they are reproduced here with her understanding of how the prayers she inspired are meant for all the members of the family of the sacred rose.

The first poem was written on her 89th birthday, 16th September 2012. You are welcome to use it for anyone whom you love to send them the glorious rose energy.

Roses Falling

Roses fall from the sky
As I look through my window
I think I am still dreaming
That we are together today
The roses cover a small patch
Of Mother Earth in my garden
They connect us
As I hear myself
Calling to you
On your day of birth
Drawing in my breath
A sharp intake
As the downfall continues
I see the magic intensify
As the rose petals
Dance on the ground now
My eyes water as I watch
This sacred display
Interfacing with the Earth Mother
The roses form generous shapes
And rose symbols
And I am amazed
My heart opens at the sight
And the rose energy
Ignites my sacred space
And yours
I send the rose energy to you
To caress your living space
To heal your body
To open the door

To your kingdoms
To create your essential self
As a living portal of roses
You are alone no more
Bereft no more
I am now conscious
Of all that I can be
And I choose that
I hope you choose it too
My choice
Made here and now
Is for the rose petals
To continue to fall
On one spot
On Mother Earth
And to bring with them
Their illumination
Their sacredness
Their joy!

And The Prayers Continue ...

Use whichever one feels light and bright for you. All of them link with the rose energy. It is up to you to choose.

The Gentle Night Watch

The gentle night watch begins
The portal is closed now
I stand before it
Attired in red
The colour of strength
I raise my sword in front of me
And watch each movement, each shiver, and each shadow
Each fragment of darkness that I encounter
I watch with interest
I repel all boarders
I judge nothing I receive everything
Yet I do deny any intruders
The right to menace those whom I love
The Rose Mother
Sleeps peacefully in her bed
Relaxed at last
After so many trials
After so much trouble
So much sadness
The depth of the sorrow
Has entered her bones
Her aura hangs in tatters
We restore that now
The Rose Archangels and I
We gather around her bed

Watching her as she sleeps
We understand her
We love her
We watch over her
And now
In the night the dreams come
The healing dreams move through her vibration
They cover her in love
And she is free of fear
And free of pain
And a new day will dawn tomorrow!

This poem was used to entice people into the change process that will take us all through into consciousness. It can be used as it stands or as a potent Declaration of Intention.

The Golden Feather

The door is waiting
It stands before us
Shaped like an enticing rose
The petals rampaging with colour
As we watch them
Shimmer in the sunlight
Offering us a new reality
And we are here
A group of potent women
Waiting to move
Into the next level
Encompassing a new dimension
Daring to be different
Removing our chains
Breaking out of captivity after centuries
Into a new reality
No longer surviving now thriving
Some sisters are leaving at this point
Choosing to run
From the energetic changes that have reached us now
They cannot face their new being
Behind me
I feel you pull away
Choosing to remain in this reality
Harnessed by business or work or family
We bid you fond farewell

And those who remain link arms
Readying themselves to walk through the door
Those who remain
Understand the collective choice
Being made now
Along the way
We have given up ourselves
We believed in our sisterhood role
And we delivered
Now we are free and the choice is ours
As individuals and as a collective
Do we go on
Do we open the door
Or remain to repeat
Old patterns interminably
Those of us who stand together
Decide to move
The door sings to us
It is calling
Hear the song and open your heart
A golden feather finds us
It is the key to the kingdom
We will now once we enter
Be all that we can be
We will open to the true depths
Of our intensity
The tears flow
We join hands
We use the key
We enter
And we choose consciousness!!

The Rose Mother

We sit around you in a circle
The Rose Women, goddesses, angels, archangels
And Rose Council members all One
We acknowledge you Rose Mother
We open you to the energy of the new dimension
You are seeking
We croon to comfort you all in unison
We develop strategies to make you
Know you are loved
And more
Honoured, respected, noticed and chosen
By us as our Rose Mother
The circle vibrates
The rhythm rocks and rises
Your cheeks are wet with tears
We banish any dark energy
From your auric vibration
We celebrate you
You have drawn the evil in
On our behalf
And helped us to destroy it
Without you we might have hesitated
We may have been snowed under
With negativity and pain and sorrow
Trying too hard
Not releasing
And then you come by
With these new lessons
For us all to learn
And so we salute you

Rose Mother
As you nestle in the womb
Of the warm rose energy
And sleep deeply
Inhaling rose perfume gently
And moving into consciousness!

The Rose Mother Embodies The Oracle

Dear Rose Mother
You are the Oracle
Who sits within your cave of power
Surrounded by your generosity
Of pure spirit
It flows from your altered being
As your rose angels gather in a sacred circle
Encompassing you
Filling you with the energy
Of divine trust
Your wisdom and joy
Spill out in return
Into the atmosphere
Fracturing known negativity
Into circles of intelligence and love
The golden rose energises
Your graceful body
And your life
In the energy of the Rose
Is at once re-born!

In our dreams we often see the ruin of past lives whilst our dreams are filled with ancient memories. Legend has it that when some left Atlantis as the ruined city burnt the Rose Mother guided them to their next place of being – to Avalon. Without her they may never have made the transition.

The Rose Mother Leaves Atlantis

Look far off to the north east
As the green water claims us
And we float away on the tide
Our long close fitting dresses
Shimmer like gossamer
Our swans-down fur
Capes of huge proportions
That protected us as Atlantis collapsed
Are swept away by insistent waves
We have left behind our youth and beauty
On this fateful journey
The Rose Mother gathers the goddesses together
And our luminosity heightens
And extends extraordinarily
As we float along together
Remembering
Wisdom deeper than the deepest ocean
Sacred words resound in our ears
We look around us as our bodies
Float in the depth of the sea
In the ocean so splendid
Teeming with life
We banter quietly between ourselves
There is nothing else to do

And then our friends join us
For this is the home of the seals
Who come to us singing and playful
On the full tide
Gathering our raggedness to their hearts
Seeing our dilemma
Seeing our Rose Mother weep for us
For all that we have lost
For the end of our home, our lives
Singing their mournful wailing song
Stirring our bruised and beaten hearts
To the core
Our new seal friends bring our souls out to play
When we who can see the fires
Of the ruined Atlantis burning still
Thought all hope had gone
They usher us now on the next stage
Of our fateful journey
They save us and take us
Carefully swimming along
Until we sense a magical boundary
Shifting like the tide
Between this world and the next
An opening occurs and we
Swim through it
Emerging cleanly, safely,
Strongly on the other side
With our oceanic friends
We stride ashore confident again
Into the centre of a beautiful circle
That rises with us from the depths
The strange haunting music that follows us

The central sun twins, then moves
Rebirthing us
Enlivening the charmed circle of pure green light
And we realise that we are here
Our Rose Mother triumphantly arrives
With her Rose Goddesses at Avalon
And our world begins again!

The Rose Mothers have the ability to fly. They see things that ordinary mortals cannot. Their ancient wisdom takes them to lands we can only imagine.

Rose Echoes

A great Rose Archangel
Gathers you in His arms
And flies with you
To the moon
On the way
High over the city
You see lights flash like jewels
You observe dark glistening lakes
A snaking river
Glints of glass
From high rise buildings
Churches and their silver towers
Gleaming in the starlight
So high are you
That you can only hear
The beating of his mighty wings
No cherubs and pink clouds here
This was reality
This was happening
Angel tracks in the heavens
You in his arms
Rising gradually towards a full moon!

Christmas Day is always a special day when we remember our Rose Mothers, their love for us and our love for them.

Rose Mothers

On Christmas Day we call to you
Rose Mothers
Our mentors and friends
You who have been watching over us
Since we arrived on Mother Earth
We know that you are with us
We feel your wings moving rhythmically
Their breeze floating above our heads
We feel comforted
At your loving presence
We celebrate your intention
To guide and protect us
And to inspire us with the knowledge
To ask the questions
To change the energetic vibrations
We have established here
Into compatibility and invincible strength
And in return
We remind you to take up your personal power
Reach to the stars and to the silver moon
And bring those energies
Into Mother Earth
For the benefit of us all
Blessings Rose Mothers one and all!

Part Four

The Future

These prayers were first inspired by individuals and then took on a special form and energy all of their own. The individuals who inspired them are imbued with a special generosity of spirit that was  irresistible to the rose. Some of them call out to the missing component of our own essential selves. And so the rose poems to take us through into the future blossom as a channel for the rose energy. They enliven everyone who comes in contact with this beauty. We thank the individuals concerned for their inspiration and support.

Calling

I call to you in my dreams
I look for you amongst the stars
I walk on rainbows to find you
You are there close by sometimes
I feel your breath upon my shoulder
I turn and you are gone
You send me pictures in my mind
Of us when we were last together
You show me glimpses
Of where you have gone to now
I can see so little
Of what you want to show me
My heart aches
My soul shudders
And then all of a sudden
Everything changes
I see you clearly now
And we can talk out loud
Not just in dreams
Any time
We can laugh together in the morning
Cry together at night
And understand what each is enduring
We have something so special
Words would ruin it
We are of one accord
In the links we foster
We generate love between the spheres
There is no separation now
We open the gates between Earth and Heaven

And nothing is ever the same again
As healing comes
Born on rose angels' wings
Filled with rose angels' blessings
And I am at last – content!

Silent Wings

Silent wings
You beat in time with me
As a new day dawns
This is the moment
When you will help me to look into his eyes
Knowing we must soon part
I surrender to his beingness
As I remember us and our commitment
Of the purest energetic vibration
Destined to be together
For the rest of our earthly lives
All other commitments
Became null and void
And were released back to the universe
We spent our days together
We communed gently
We marvelled at the links we found
When we talked quietly of days gone by
And now that they are ending
I salute him
I see his eyes dim and darken
I watch him wander ahead of me to another place
I know he will be there
When I come through
The Tunnel of Light
However the ease leaves me
My hands tremble
My brow furrows
And I weep for the loss of my true friend
I feel the loneliness

Envelope me like a blanket
And then you come
With your sweet silent wings
You fold me in your arms
And I relax into nothingness
And I am yours.

Watching

I watch for your love
As each day passes
Into night
Like a miser I hoard it
When I feel it coming
Across the seas

I touch your energy
Differently now
Yet still you are there
Watching out for me
I feel you at odd times
And I embrace you
Love of my life
When will we meet again?

A Blue River Of Love

A blue river of love
Flows from my soul into yours
It rushes through your body
Healing all ills with its warmth
It plays within your DNA
Pushing out anything that does not belong
Gently oh so gently
And transmutes it
Increasing your level of wellness
And pure vitality
A Blue River of love
Galvanises your immunity
To all ills
It teases you and moves you
With its flirting flamboyance
And as this Blue River of love comes
Breathe deeply into it
For as it enters your system
The two of us unite
And you are healed.

Communion

Your eyes look
Into the depths of mine
Promising reunion soon
They reassure me
As I touch your hand
Quietly and slowly
My fingers lingering on yours
The longing in them
Reaching in to every fibre
Of your special being
You touch my lips
With one finger
Quieting me
As I try to talk
Too much
And so I relax against you
Our bodies generating more heat
Between us
Although we have barely touched
We walk together
A couple at last
Through the city streets
Oblivious of noise
Of traffic
Of people
For this is our world
And we are its only inhabitants!

The Bridge Of Living Roses

The Bridge of Living Roses
Pulses from my side
Of this sacred island
To your door
Never have I seen such a sight
It is luminous bright and light
The roses are vigorous and strong
They are insistent that you are the one
This living bridge they whisper
In hushed tones
Is not frequently used
It is pulsed
At times of great importance
When a new phase is begun
For someone
Whose place in the scheme
Is profound
You can call them to you
For extra enlightenment
If you wish- call now
In a light filled voice
Rose bridge, come to me
Bridge Roses
And they will unfurl
Their huge forms gradually reveal themselves
An insistent whispering
Accompanying them
As they move into your space.
Feel them form a circle of comfort
Around you

You who have worked so hard
And accomplished so much
Dance with them now
They will calibrate
A new form of rose consciousness
For you to feel in this world
Feel the sensation
Of weightlessness and pure love
They bring
And do your divine work now
On this Bridge of Living Roses.

The Rose Ladder

You wake in the night
Your brow furrowed with puzzlement
Your body twitches
As you wait quietly in your bed
Your mind expands
And then they are there
The roses singing in harmony
Your heavenly link
Surrounding you with love
Suddenly in the corner of your room
A ladder of roses is illuminated
Its place in the corner of your room
Shining and secure
And then you see her
The Rose Archangel
She descends
She turns and sits
On the ladder's bottom rung
And coolly she observes you
The rose guard is changing
She comments
As if you have been constantly
Conversing
I am your new rose friend
A partner in your healing
You are in awe and amazed
As you watch her every move
My contribution to you is
Pre-ordained she continues
Her breath a whisper on the wind

And in no doubt she murmurs
And the rose essence of her
Fills the air with perfume
Reaching into your nostrils
Healing gentling expanding
She unfurls her rainbow wings
In a light display
Unprecedented
Your eyes like saucers
You watch
The generative rose energy
Clambers around the room
So strongly
It seems to resonate
In every corner and crevice
Your DNA zings with expectation
You open your essential self
To change
The roses dance wildly now
Building to a crescendo
You watch your eyes like saucers
You see her smile
And the smile opens your soul
To the rose
An orchestra seems to play
In the background
You are aware
You notice everything
And suddenly all is quiet
The tears fall freely
And you
Vibrate consciousness

As the rose ladder vanishes
Into the night
Sure to come again tomorrow!

The Closing Pattern Of The Rose

As I thank the Rose Council
for appearing in all its beauty and power,
I ignite my luminous body from the acceptance of my divinity.

From within the vastness of my inner Sun, I birth potential worlds.

My personal Tree of Life glistens with anticipation,
love and unadulterated power.
Its roses blossom into rainbows and reach out into the sky.
Within the foundation of my human form
I awaken my star essence,
touching gently all worlds and all beings.

Feathers caress my inner and outer being.
My inner Sun blazes with unconditional love.
I feel the radiance of my embodied Moon.
I taste its brilliance.

I express my gratitude to the Rose Council
for activating change, healing those named
and protecting those who are vulnerable.

The time is now.

A Rose Postscript

If you have enjoyed the Rose Prayers you may find that the next step on the rose journey is to explore the sacred journeys and meditations of the rose.

Books on these topics can be downloaded from my website at www.roseseichim.com

These journeys can take you to those wonderful creative places where change and inspiration await to transform you. Or you might enjoy a rose record reading in the form of a consultation of the rose akashic records, details of which are also on my website.

If you wish to have a special sacred rose poem designed for yourself or someone close to you please contact me.

About The Author

Dr. Christine (Cris) Henderson is an international Creativity Consultant and through her business, Crescendo Solutions, she is helping people to change with ease.

Cris holds a Ph.D. in International Relations and an M.A. from Queensland University. She attended the Universities of Warwick and Oxford completing courses in university administration, as well as the Darden School of Business Administration, and the University of Virginia, participating in a high level course in strategic alliances. She lived for six years in Hong Kong gaining an understanding and appreciation of Asian business and culture. She has also qualified as a Master Trainer in Reiki and Seichim.

She is currently a dedicated carer for her husband who is, with her vital assistance, successfully recovering from a severe stroke.

Amongst her credits are "A Work of Faith - The History of The Glennie School, Toowoomba", which traces the history of women's education in Queensland, and "Cancer Help" published by Simon and Schuster in two editions. The subject of her latest books, "Seichim: the Magic of Seichim Energy Training", "Reiki Inside Out", and "Rose Alchemy" is energy training. "Mini Meditations" were first published on an occasional basis in 'Insight Magazine', and in New Zealand in 'In Touch Magazine' and 'Rainbow News.'

Cris is a "people person" who is recognized as an initiator of change. She specializes in writing workbooks, courses and articles tailored to benefit the individual needs of the reader. As an innovator and writer she focuses on assisting individuals to achieve their fullest potential in the face of challenge and change.

For further information please contact Cris on 61-7-3410-1194 or by writing to PO Box 1207 Bongaree, Bribie Island, 4507, Australia or e-mail crishendo1@bigpond.com

Printed in Great Britain
by Amazon

19742547R00071